THE FASTEST

FASCINATING FACTS

David Armentrout

The Rourke Press, Inc.
Vero Beach, Florida 32964

6839658

PHOTO CREDITS
© Tommy Dodson: pg. 10; © Warren Faidley/Int'l Stock: pg 12;
© Michele & Tom Grimm/Int'l Stock: pg. 13; © Gayln C.
Hammond: pg. 15; © Michael J. Howell/Int'l Stock: Right Cover,
pg. 17; © Joe McDonald: Left Cover, pg. 4; © Howard Paulman:
pg. 18; © David Rucker: pg. 7; © Sanford/Agliolo/Int'l Stock: Title
page; © 1996 Sea World of Florida, All Rights Reserved: pg. 8;
© Doris VanBuskirk: pg. 21

Library of Congress Cataloging-in-Publication Data

Armentrout, David, 1962–
    The fastest / David Armentrout.
       p. cm. — (Fascinating facts)
    ISBN 1-57103-127-8
    Summary: Brief presentations of facts about some of the fastest
things on Earth.
    1. Speed—Juvenile literature. [1. Speed.]
I. Title II. Series: Armentrout, David, 1962- Fascinating facts.
QC127.4.A76 1996
031.02—dc20
                                      96–25730
                                        CIP
                                        AC

Printed in the USA

TABLE OF CONTENTS

ANIMAL

Over short distances, no animal on Earth outruns the cheetah. This large member of the cat family sprints at almost 70 miles an hour.

The cheetah is an **endangered species** (en DAYN jerd) (SPEE sheez), which means very few are left in the wild. The cheetah can still be found in small numbers in tropical Africa, where it lives on open plains.

Cheetahs **prey** (PRAY) on large animals such as wildebeests, gazelles, and impala. They are good hunters and catch about half the animals they chase.

Over short distances, no animal can catch the cheetah

AIRCRAFT

One military airplane goes on record as the fastest jet aircraft: the Lockheed SR-71 Blackbird.

The record-breaking speed occurred on July 28, 1976. Captain Joersz and Major Morgan flew at 2,193 miles an hour. That's more than three times the speed of sound!

The first SR-71 Blackbird flight took place in 1958. The Blackbirds were used to survey, or spy on, enemy lands. The Air Force retired the Jets in 1989 to save money.

The now-retired SR-71 Blackbird is the fastest jet aircraft on record

SEA MAMMAL

The orca, or killer whale, is the largest member of the dolphin family. Of all the mammals in the sea, none swims faster than the mighty killer whale. One male orca was timed at 34 miles an hour!

Killer whales may also be the world's best **predator** (PRED uh ter), or hunter, of other creatures. They are smart and often hunt together. Killer whales feed on fish, squids, seals, and penguins. Killer whales have even been known to prey on blue whales, the largest creatures on Earth.

In captivity, the killer whale has proven to be a friendly, curious animal

BIRD

With a bullet-shaped body and long, pointed wings, the **peregrine falcon** (PER uh grin) (FAL kun) flies nearly 200 miles an hour! This bird of prey—maybe the world's fastest—reaches top speed when it dives for a snake or other small animal.

The peregrine falcon catches its victim with sharp claws; but it makes the kill with its sharp, powerful beak.

The peregrine falcon's bullet-shaped body and strong wings enable it to fly faster than any other bird

The wind speed inside a hurricane has been clocked at over 200 miles an hour

Riding a skateboard takes balance

PLANT

Most plants grow very slowly, but not bamboo. Some bamboo plants grow 24 inches a day to a height of 164 feet. In fact, bamboo is the fastest growing plant.

People use bamboo to build houses and furniture and to make baskets and musical instruments. You may even have used a bamboo fishing pole.

The endangered giant panda is an animal that depends on bamboo for survival. This cuddly looking bear eats bamboo shoots and lives in the bamboo forests of central China.

Some types of bamboo grow two feet a day

TRAIN

A railroad train is pulled by an engine, or **locomotive** (LO kuh MO tiv). The first locomotives were steam-powered. Today steam, diesel, and electric locomotives are used all over the world.

The fastest passenger trains are in France. The high-speed trains have front and rear electric locomotives that are controlled by computers.

An electric passenger train set a speed record in 1990 when it traveled at 320 miles an hour!

French high-speed trains are the world's fastest, smoothest trains

PASSENGER PLANE

A supersonic aircraft flies faster than the speed of sound. The Concorde is the fastest passenger jet of all.

The Concorde cruises at 1,450 miles an hour. It can fly from New York to London in 2 hours 54 minutes. Most airliners take two or three times longer to make that trip.

To fly this fast, the Concorde uses twice as much fuel as a regular airliner. It is also very noisy, and many airports will not allow it to land. Unless these problems are overcome, the Concorde will not be used much.

The "nose" of the Concorde airliner is shaped for high speed

SNAKE

The mamba snake is the most feared snake in Africa. Among the fastest of all snakes, the bold mamba has been known to chase and bite people. A mamba's venom, or poison, can kill a person in minutes.

The mamba is part of the cobra family, but it does not have the hood that makes other cobras look fierce.

The mamba lives and hunts in trees; but the black mamba, which can grow to 14 feet, also hunts on the ground.

In short bursts, the mamba snake zips along at 12 miles an hour

SKATEBOARD

Skateboarding came from roller skating. The first boards were wooden planks with roller skate wheels attached.

Riding a skateboard takes balance. The most skilled skateboard riders can turn, spin forward and backward, skate on their hands, and jump.

The fastest recorded speed on a skateboard is over 78 miles an hour. Other records include a high jump over 5 feet and a ride of more than 270 miles.

Glossary

endangered species (en DAYN jerd) (SPEE sheez) — a kind of animal in danger of no longer existing

locomotive (LO kuh MO tiv) — a car used to move railroad cars; an engine

peregrine falcon (PER uh grin) (FAL kun) — a swift long-winged hawk with gray and white feathers

predator (PRED uh ter) — animals that hunt other animals for food

prey (PRAY) — an animal that is hunted by another animal for food

INDEX